Contents

1: Fake LO♥E
(Amore Falso)

2: Serve or Control?
(Servire o Controllare?)

3: Live & Let Live
(Vivi e Lascia Vivere)

4: Fucking
(Scopiamo)

5: Metamorphosis
(Metamorfosi)

6: Panic Attack
(Attacco di Panico)

7: Domestication is Not Your Thing
(L'addomesticamento Non Fa Per Te)

8: The Naughty Santa
(Il Cattivo Babbo Natale)

9: I Wasn't Born a Boy!
(Non Sono Nato Maschio!)

10: The Pull of the Flesh
(L'attrazione della Carne)

11: Suck My Clit
(Succhiami il Clitoride)

12: The Last Supper
(L'ultima Cena)

13: Never Felt So Alive
(Non Mi Sono Mai Sentito Così Vivo)

14: You've Got Spirit
(Hai Spirito)

15: I've Thrown It Back to The Universe
(L'ho Ributtato nell'Universo)

16: Consciousness
(Coscienza)

17: The Phoenix
(La Fenice)

Contents

18: Lo♥e Hole
(Buco dell'Amore)

19: If a Man Didn't Have a Cock!
(Se un Uomo non Avesse il Cazzo)

20: For "Preety"
(Per "Preety")

21: Moses & The Promised Land
(Mosè e la Terra Promessa)

22: Sex & Friendship
(Sesso e Amicizia)

23: Child of the Universe
(Figlia dell'Universo)

24: The Elder
(L'anziano)

25: Are You Experienced?
(Hai Esperienza?)

26: Nettie

27: Times
(I Tempi)

28: Whatever Gets You Through the Night (Is Alright!)
(Qualunque Cosa ti Faccia Passare la Notte (Va Bene!))

29: How Old Are You?
(Quanti Anni Hai?)

30: Manipulation
(Manipolazione)

31: Stella
(Star)

32: Structure
(Struttura)

33: Better Out Than In
(Meglio Fuori Che Dentro)

34: The "Why Not" Attitude
(L'atteggiamento del "Perché No")

Acknowledgement of Land & of the Traditional Owners of this Land

I would like to acknowledge the Gadigal people of the Eora Nation, upon whose stolen land I stand on today.
I recognise that this land was never terra nullius — the land belonging to these peoples was never ceded, given up, bought or sold.
I would like to pay my respects to Aboriginal Elders past, present and emerging, and I extend this acknowledgement to all Aboriginal and Torres Strait Islander people.

Rainy Day Women #12 & 35

"Well, they'll stone you when you're trying to be so good
They'll stone you just like they said they would
They'll stone you when you're trying to go home
And they'll stone you when you're there all alone
But I would not feel so all alone
Everybody must get stoned.

Well, they'll stone you when you're walking on the street
They'll stone you when you're tryin' to keep your seat
They'll stone you when you're walkin' on the floor
They'll stone you when you're walkin' to the door
But I would not feel so all alone
Everybody must get stoned.

They'll stone you when you're at the breakfast table
They'll stone you when you are young and able
They'll stone you when you're tryin' to make a buck
Then they'll stone you and then they'll say "good luck"
Tell ya what, I would not feel so all alone
Everybody must get stoned.

Well, they'll stone you and say that it's the end
Then they'll stone you and then they'll come back again
They'll stone you when you're riding in your car
They'll stone you when you're playing your guitar
Yes, but I would not feel so all alone
Everybody must get stoned alright.

Well, they'll stone you when you walk all alone
They'll stone you when you are walking home
They'll stone you and then say you are brave
They'll stone you when you are set down in your grave
But I would not feel so all alone
Everybody must get stoned."

Songwriter: Bob Dylan

Contents

35: Do Not Seek the Treasure
(Non Cercare il Tesoro)
36: The Perfect Gentleman
(Il Perfetto Gentiluomo)
37: I'll Be the Judge of That
(Sarò il Giudice di Questo)
38: I Wish
(Spero che)
39: Low
(Basso)
40: Acknowledgement
(Riconoscimento)
41: We Were Born to Die
(Siamo Nati per Morire)
42: Shadows in the Night
(Ombre Nella Notte)
43: Suffering
(Sofferenza)
44: We Were Born to Live
(Siamo Nati per Vivere)
45: In-Sane
(In-Sano di Mente)
46: Fantasy & Reality
(Fantasia e Realtà)
47: I Am a Spirit in the Material World
(Sono Uno Spirito nel Mondo Materiale)
48: Humanise Yourself
(Umanizzare te Stesso)
49: A Hopeful Human
(Un Umano Pieno di Speranza)
50: We Can be LO♥ERS but We Cannot Be Friends
(Possiamo essere Amanti ma non Possiamo essere Amici)

Fake LO♥E

(Amore Falso)

You know the kind.
We've all experienced it.
We've all dealt with it.
We've all lived with it.
We've all lived through it.
We've all put up with it.
Fake LO♥E.

It's a LO♥E which is difficult.
It's a LO♥E which is hard work.
It's a LO♥E which makes you ask yourself...
..."Is this all worth it?"
It's a LO♥E where you ask yourself one day...
..."What am I doing here?"
This is Fake LO♥E.

But yet we put up with it.
We go on with our lives with it.
Why do we stay?
Why do we do it?
Is it loyalty?
Is it fear?
Is delusional?
Is it narcissism?
Is it ego?
Why do waste away our lives with...
...Fake LO♥E?

"The Don"
01.08.2021

Serve or Control?

(Servire o Controllare?)

Do People *"Serve"* or *"Control"*?
What is the role of politicians?
What is the function of a government?
In a *"supposed"* Democracy...
...I thought they were elected to *"Serve"*.
...To carry out the *"Will of the People"*.
Apparently, I was wrong.
They instead, decide for us.
They *"Control"* us.
Do people "Serve" or "Control"?

Governments no longer *"Serve"* the People.
The People *"Serve"* them.
We no longer *"Control"* politicians & governments.
They *"Control"* us.
People no longer are in *"Control"*.
People now *"Serve"*.
Power has shifted.
Do People "Serve" or Control"?

"Well, we know the answer to that, don't we?"

"We "Serve"!"

Politicians do not *"Serve"* us.
Governments do not *"Serve"* us.
Politicians *"Control'* us.
Governments *"Control"* us.

"The Don"
02.08.2021

Live & Let Live

(Vivi e Lascia Vivere)

Be & let be.
Do & let do.
Say & let say.
Dance & let dance.
Sing & let sing.
Drink & let drink.
Party & let party.
Fly & let fly.
Pray & let pray.
Create & let create.
Enjoy & let enjoy.
Cry & let cry.
Scream & let scream.
Lay & let lay.
Fuck & let fuck.
LO♥E & let LO♥E.
Die & let die.
Live & let live.

"The Don"
02.08.2021

Fucking

(Scopiamo)

Fucking, what a weird act.
When you stop & think about it...
...it's a pretty insane idea.
...insert a part of your body into another person.
...whoever thought of that must have been out of their fucking heads.
... it's such a bizarre idea.
...to copulate.
...to procreate.
Yet all mammals do it.
And its only mammals that *FUCK*.

I'm sure there are easier ways to do it.
Let's take fish for example...
...theirs' is very simple & straight forward.
...the female lays her eggs on a rock or something similar.
...the male comes along & sprays his semen over them.
...quick, simple, efficient.
...no mess.
...no insertion of body parts from one gender to the other.
...very impersonal.
...very sterile.
...very clinical.
...very straightforward.
No *FUCKING* involved here.

For mammals on the other hand & especially humans...
...*fucking is very messy.*
...*fucking is very awkward.*
...*insertion can be difficult.*
...*the position is not very comfortable.*
...*the vagina is in an awkward location.*
...*the woman has to spread her legs very wide apart.*
...*the man has to straddle her in some way.*
... *either by laying on top of her, in the traditional "Missionary Position".*
...*or some other exotic position.*
...*all quite cumbersome & uncomfortable to say the least.*
...*for both participants.*
...*it would have been much easier if it was located where the bellybutton is, for example.*
So, fucking certainly is a weird act, when you stop & think about.
"But who stops & thinks about?"
"Not me!"

Artist: Preet Kaur Nanak

"The Don"
02.08.2021

Metamorphosis

(Metamorfosi)

Change is good.

Change is necessary.

Rebirth is good.

Rebirth is necessary.

Regeneration is good.

Regeneration is necessary.

Transformation is good.

Transformation is necessary.

Evolution is good.

Evolution is necessary.

Metamorphosis!

"The Don"
04.08.2021

Panic Attack

(Attacco di Panico)

I had a panic attack.
The "Bastard" came back.
He was on my back.
He was on my track.
I should never look back.
It was another setback.
I was on the right track.
It had laid a trap.
It was just having a nap.
Then it had a snack.
Now it's back.
I nearly had a heart attack.
He's on my back.
I know it's a setback.
I was on the right track.
But...
...the "Bastard" came back.
I had a panic attack.

It's another setback.
I thought I was on the right track.
But the "Bastard's" come back.
I had a panic attack.

Panic attack!
Panic attack!
Panic attack!
Panic attack!

"I got my wiring crossed!"
"I guess I blew a fuse!"

"The Don"
06.08.2021

Domestication is Not Your Thing

(L'addomesticamento Non Fa Per Te)

Domestication is not your thing.
You've tried it many times.
You've given it a good shot.
You've tried your best.
You've put your whole heart into it.
But domestication is not your thing.

You've been married twice.
You've had many relationships.
You've had many LO❤ERS.
You've tried it many times.
You've given it a good shot.
You've tried your best.
But domestication is not your thing.

You told me, *"I want to be a housewife!"*
"I want to live in a mansion!"
Live in a mansion, but you're no housewife!
You've tried it many times.
You've given it a good shot.
You've tried your best.
But domestication is not your thing.

You're too wild!
You're too crazy!
You're too FREE!
You cannot be tamed!
You can be tied down!
You're a real *"Wild Child"*!
You've tried it many times.
You've given it a good shot.
You've tried your best.
But domestication is not your thing.

"Forget it!"
"Domestication is not your thing'.

"But don't worry..."
"...It's not mine either!"

"The Don"
07.08.2021

The Naughty Santa

(Il Cattivo Babbo Natale)

He'll come in through your window.
He'll come in through your door.
He'll come in when you're sleeping.
He'll come into your bed, if he's invited.
He'll make LO♥E to you.
Then leave you a present...
He is *"The Naughty Santa"*.

He's been around for centuries.
He is known by many names...
...Casanova.
...Rasputin.
...Don Juan.
...The Marquis de Sade.
...Don Giovanni.
...The Devil.
He'll make LO♥E to you.
Then leave you a present...
...if you've been naughty too.
He is *"The Naughty Santa"*.

He is as cuddly as a teddy bear.
He is as cute as a puppy dog.
He is as LO♥ABLE as a Meerkat.
He is a playful as a pussycat.
He is magical as the stars in the sky.
He is as whimsical as the gossamer wind.
He is as romantic as the moon.
He'll make LO♥E to you.
Then leave you a present.
He is *"The Naughty Santa"*.

"The Don"
08.08.2021

"The Don"
(The Naughty Santa)

I Wasn't Born a Boy!

(Non Sono Nato Maschio!)

It's s travesty.
It's a tragedy.
It's s horror story.
It's a nightmare.
If you're not wanted.
If you're not LO♥ED.
If you're not what they wanted.
If you're shunned.
If you're rejected.
If you're abandoned.
Because you weren't born a boy.
Because you were born a girl instead.

It wasn't your fault.
You are not to blame.
You didn't have a choice in the matter.
You weren't asked if you wanted to be born a boy.
Shit, you weren't asked a fucking thing.
You were just born.
With a *"Moon & Star"* on your head.
They didn't see this.
An innocent child.
Born into a hateful world.
You were not wanted.
You were shunned.
You were rejected.
You were abandoned.
You were not LO♥ED.
Because you weren't born a boy.
Because you were born a girl instead.

He wanted a boy.
They wanted a boy.
But you were born a girl.
A girl in a *"man's world"*!
A *"man's world"* is no place for a girl.

"I'm sorry I wasn't a boy!"

"You've got nothing to be sorry for!"
"It's not your fault!"

"The Don"
08.08.2021

The Pull of the Flesh

(L'attrazione della Carne)

"The Pull of the Flesh"...
...is one fucking force.
It has one "Mother of a fucker" bunch.
It will knock you out.
Don't understand estimate its power.
You have no "Fucking" chance.
From "The Pull of the Flesh".

It's gut wrenching.
It sends tremors all through your body.
It is relentless.
Its pull is a force of nature.
Can you withstand its power?
Can you defeat "The Pull of the Flesh"?

It's as traumatic as being pushed out of your mother's womb.
It's as traumatic as the very first breath of this toxic planet.
It's as toxic as being slapped on the bum for the very first time.
It's as traumatic as your umbilical cord being cut from your mother's body.
This the trauma of "The Pull of the Flesh".

It's like a hand is ripping out your insides.
It's like you are about die from asphyxiation.
It's as if your heart is out of control.
It's like your whole body is about to explode.
This is the feeling of the trauma of "The Pull of the Flesh".

Symptoms to look out for include, but are not limited to...
...heart palpitations.
...shivering.
...shaking all over.
...trembling.
...panic attacks.
Any of these & you're suffering "The Pull of the Flesh".

"It's brutal!"

"The Don"
08.08.2021

Suck My Clit

(Succhiami il Clitoride)

I am intelligent.
I am beautiful.
I am cultured.
I was born to pleasure men.
It's time to spread my legs.
Come to mama.
Suck my Clit.

Let me have my moment.
Let me enjoy my time.
I know I am powerful.
I know I have energy.
I know people can't handle me.
I was born to pleasure men.
It's time to spread my legs.
Come to mama.
Suck my Clit.

I have this effect on men.
I have power.
I am an enchantress.
I am temptress.
I will give you a *"boner"*.
You won't stand a chance.
I was born to pleasure men.
It's time to spread my legs.
Come to mama.
Suck my Clit.

"I have a "boner"!"

"You're tripping!"

"The Don"
10.08.2021

Artist: Preet Kaur Nanak
Insta: preetkaurnanak

The Last Supper

(L'ultima Cena)

You brought your music book.
You played piano.
I cooked your dinner.
You were part of my family.
You said you'd never experienced this before.
You were happy.
It was the last supper.

We got drunk.
We got stoned.
We listened to music.
I played you *"Traveling Lady"* by Leonard Cohen.
You said that you LO♥ED it.
That it was perfect.
I played it for you.
I put my HE♥RT & soul into it
I think you felt it.
That was the last supper.

I made my stand.
I told you my feelings.
I revealed my HE♥RT.
"You can't just pick & choose parts of me".
"I come as a complete package".
"This is who I am".
"My feelings for you will never change".
That was the last supper.

I made it clear.
I had to do it.
I had to tell her.
That this was the last supper.

"I can't give you what you want babe".
"I can't give you what you need babe".
"I'm not the one you are looking for babe!"

"Go away from my window
Leave at your own chosen speed
I'm not the one you want, babe
I'm not the one you need

You say you're lookin' for someone
Who's never weak but always strong
To protect you and defend you
Whether you are right or wrong
Someone to open each and every door
But it ain't me, babe
No, no, no, it ain't me, babe
It ain't me you're lookin' for, babe

Go lightly from the ledge, babe
Go lightly on the ground
I'm not the one you want, babe
I will only let you down

You say you're lookin' for someone
Who will promise never to part
Someone to close his eyes for you
Someone to close his heart
Someone who will die for you and more
But it ain't me, babe
No, no, no, it ain't me babe
It ain't me you're lookin' for, babe

Go melt back in the night
Everything inside is made of stone
There's nothing in here moving
And anyway, I'm not alone

You say you're looking for someone
Who'll pick you up each time you fall
To gather flowers constantly
And to come each time you call
A lover for your life and nothing more
But it ain't me, babe
No, no, no, it ain't me, babe
It ain't me you're lookin' for, babe."

Songwriter: Bob Dylan

"The Don"
13.08.2021

Never Felt So Alive

(Non Mi Sono Mai Sentito Così Vivo)

I felt *strong*.
I felt *powerful*.
I felt *invincible*.
I felt *immortal*.
I felt like a "Force of Nature".
I felt "The Universe".
I felt "The Energy".
I felt "The Force".
I felt LO♥E.
I felt *Human*.
I never felt so ALIVE.

I felt "The Magical".
I felt "The Mysterious".
I felt "The Oneness".
I felt "The Completeness".
I felt "The Whole".
I felt like a "Free SPIRIT".
I never felt so ALIVE.

"The Don"
13.08.2021

You've Got Spirit

(Hai Spirito)

You've got *fire*.
You've got *energy*.
You've got *magnetism*.
You've got *"The Force*.
You've got *Spirit*.

You've got *"The Light"*.
You've got an *"Aura"*.
You've got *"The Sign"*.
You've got *"The Dazzling Beauty"*.
You've got *"The Ethereal*.
You've got *Spirit*.

You've got *VITALITY*.
You've got *STRENGTH*.
You've got *POWER*.
You've got *CHARISMA*.
You've got *SPIRIT*.

Artist: Preet Kaur Nanak
Insta: preetkaurnanak

"The Don"
13.08.2021

I've Thrown It Back to The Universe
(L'ho Ributtato nell'Universo)

Let it deal with it.
Let it ride the gravity waves of The Universe.
Let it fly through *"The Cosmos"*.
Let it's *"Gosamma Wings"* glide to *"The End of Time"*.
Because...
...*I've Thrown It Back to The Universe.*

"The Don"
13.08.2021

Consciousness

(Coscienza)

How *did it come about?*
How *was it created?*
How *did it evolve?*
How *does it arise?*
How *is it formed?*
How *is it generated?*
Consciousness sets me free!
Consciousness is the way to BE!
Consciousness!

What *is its purpose?*
What *takes place?*
What *happens?*
What *creates that spark?*
What *ignites that flame?*
What *produces that fire?*
What *makes my SOUL?*
What *gives rise to ME?*
What *makes me?*
Consciousness sets me free!
Consciousness is the way to BE!
Consciousness!

"The Don"
14.08.2021

The Phoenix

(La Fenice)

What will arise?
What will follow?
What will happen?
What will transpire?
When will The Phoenix arises?

What happens after *"The Fire"*?
What happens when *"The Fire"* stops burning?
What happens when *"The Fire"* goes out?
What happens then?
What happens when The Phoenix arises?

When The Phoenix arises from "The Fire"?
When The Phoenix arises from The Ashes?
When The Phoenix arises from The Firmament?
When The Phoenix arises from The Abyss?
When The Phoenix arises from "The Hellmouth"?
What happens when The Phoenix arises?

When The Phoenix arises!
When The Phoenix arises!
When The Phoenix arises!
When The Phoenix arises!
When The Phoenix arises!

"The Don"
14.08.2021

Lo♥e Hole

(Buco dell'Amore)

Let me see.
Let me look.
Let me touch.
Let me caress.
Let me kiss.
Let me lick.
Let me suck.
Let me bite.
Let me enter.
Your LO♥E Hole.

LO♥E Hole.

LO♥E Hole.

LO♥E Hole.

LO♥E Hole!!!!!!!!

"The Don"
15.08.2021

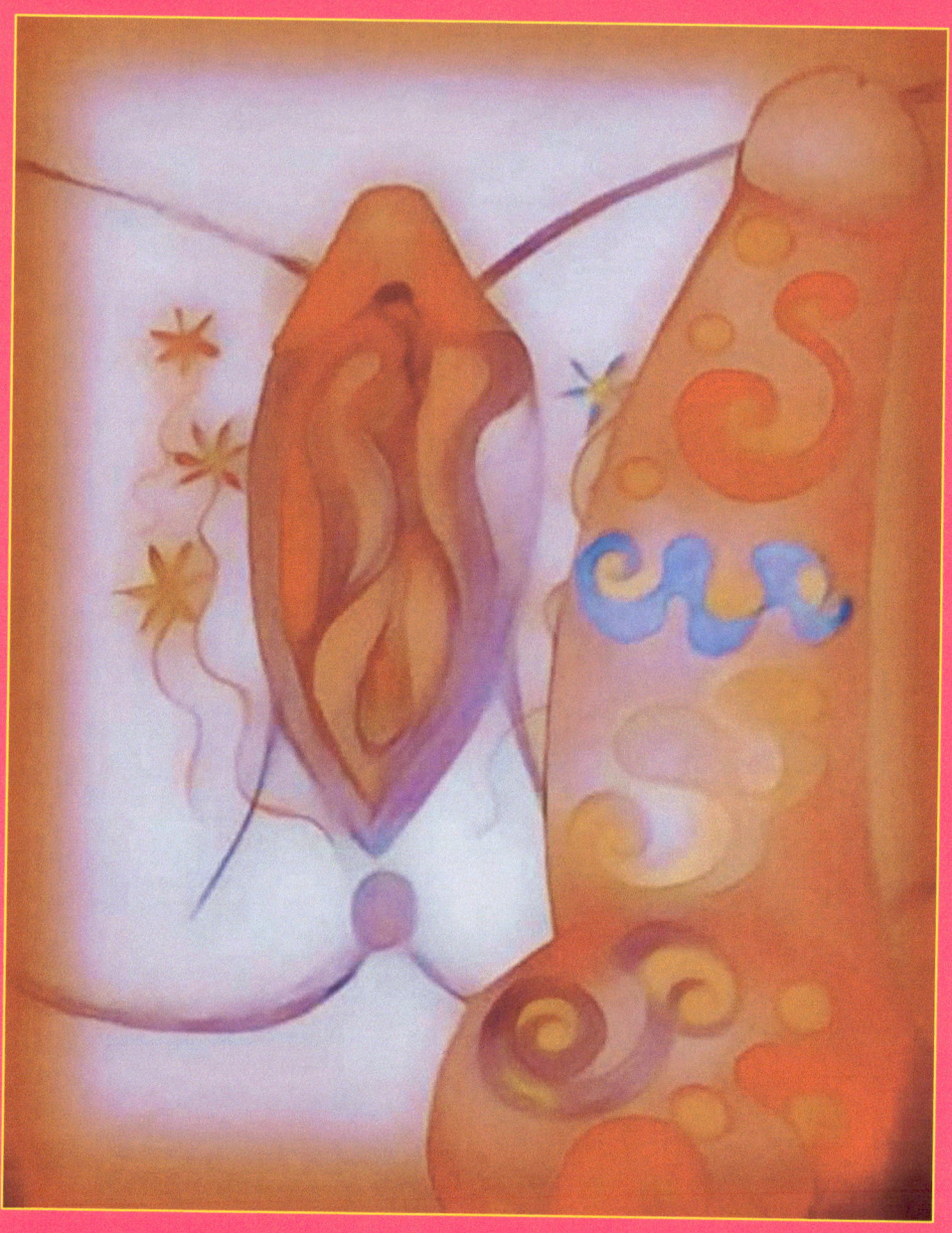

"Love Hole"
Artist: Preet Kaur Nanak
Insta: preetkaurnanak

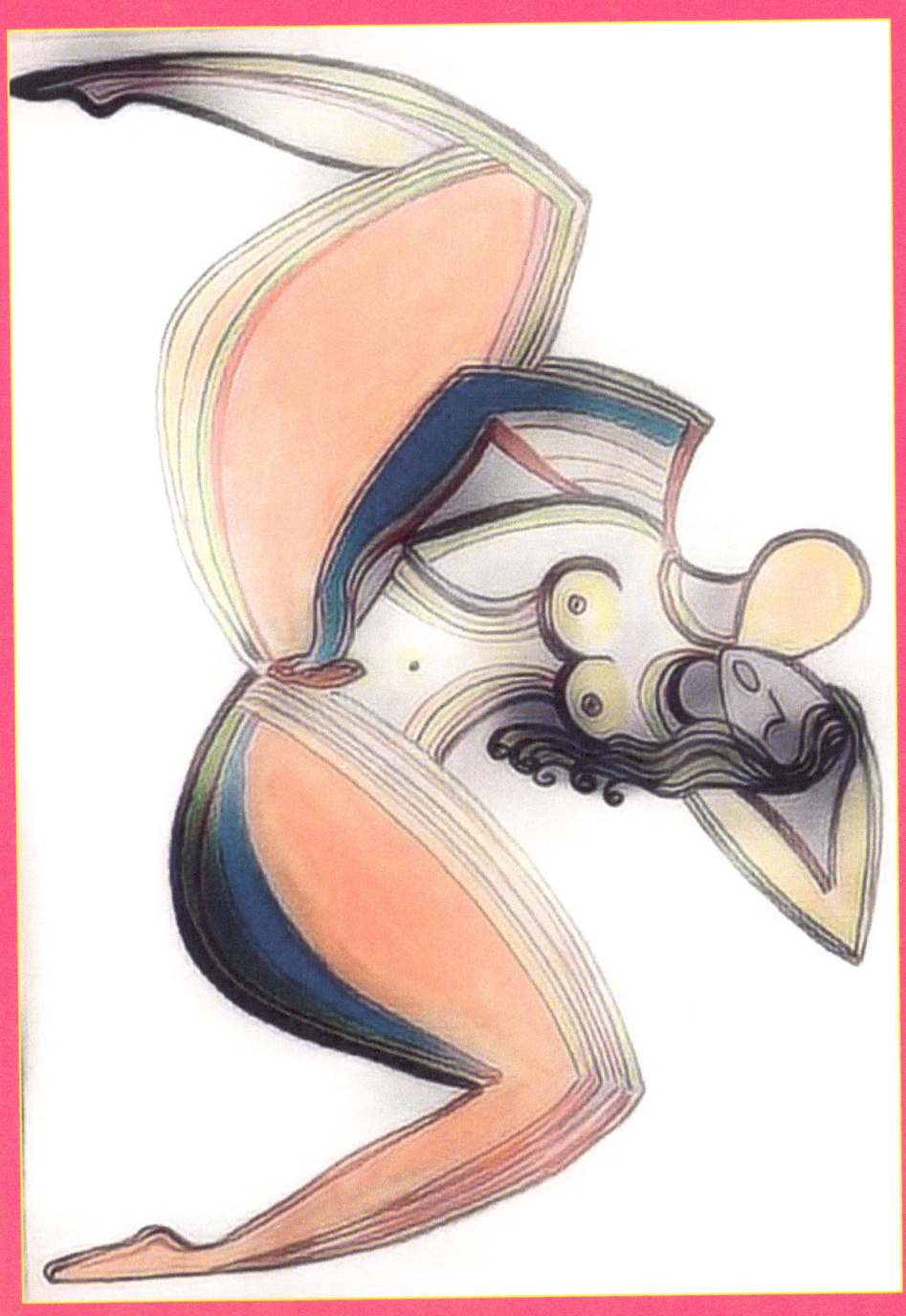

"Love Hole #2"
Artist: Preet Kaur Nanak
Insta: preetkaurnanak

If a Man Didn't Have a Cock!
(Se un Uomo non Avesse il Cazzo)

How would it be?
How would things be different?
Would things be any different?
Or would they be the same?
Would we be better off?
Would a guy be better off?
Would a girl be better off?
Would society be better off?
Would life be better off?
Would we be better off?
If...
...a man didn't have a cock?

Would his brain be wired differently?
Would he think differently?
Would he act differently?
Would he behave differently?
Would he feel differently?
Would he LO♥E differently?
If...
...a man didn't have a cock?

Would we have a different kind of politician?
Would we have a different kind government?
Would we have a different System?
Would we have a different Establishment?
Would we have a different SOCIETY?
Would we have a different FUTURE?
If...
...a man didn't have a cock?

"The Don"
15.08.2021

"Tattooed Cock"
Artist: Preet Kaur Nanak
Insta: preetkaurnanak

For "Preety"

(Per "Preety")

I call her *"Preety"*.
I call her beautiful.
I call her gorgeous.
I call her *"SuPeR SEXY babe"*.
Her name is *"Preet"*.
But I call her "Preety".

She lives in Argentina.
She is an artist.
She paints with her body, sometimes.
She is SENSUAL.
She is SEXY.
She is BEAUTIFUL.
She is my beautiful "Preety".

I have never met her in person.
Not yet anyway.
I don't know what her name means.
I don't know where it comes from.
I know that I LO♥E her.
I know that she is my *"Soulmate"*.
I know I will meet her someday.
My LO♥ELY "Preety".

She has many LO♥ERS.
I know of at least three.
There's Rasputin, Robert & Alcides.
They all want to make LO♥E to her.
And who wouldn't!
My adorable "Preety".

She is so desirable & delectable.
Even edible.
I have a fight on my hands that's for sure.
But I am a LO♥ER not a fighter I told her.
I am a humble poet.
I only have words to fight with.
Will that be enough to...
...*win over adorable "Preety"?*

She can dance too.
I think that's what attracted me to her first.
She has ALL the moves.
She is *VERY PRETTY!*
My faraway "Preety".

Artist: Preet Kaur Nanak (Insta: preetkaurnanak)

"The Don"
16.08.2021

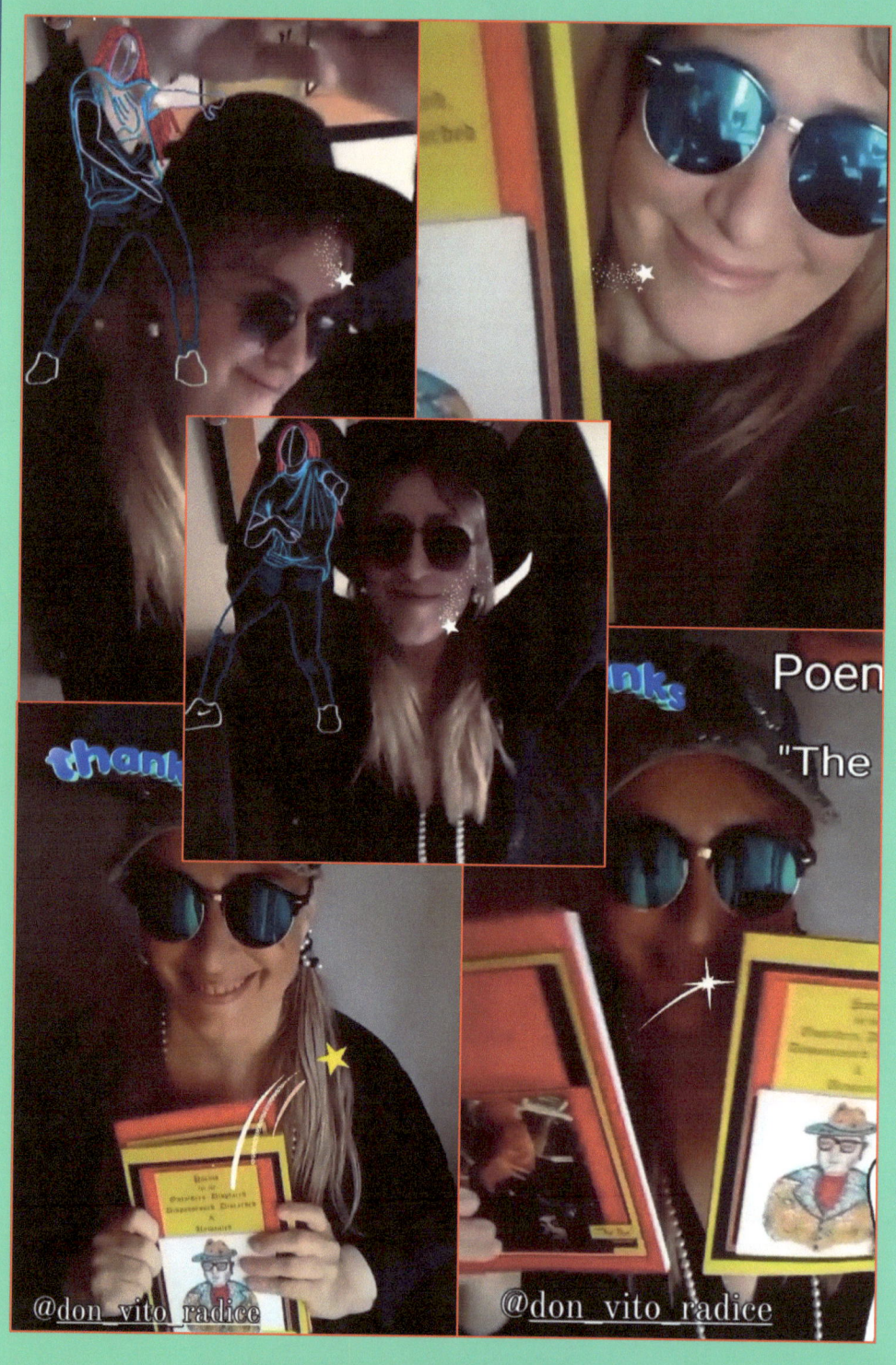

"Preety"
Preet Kaur Nanak
Insta: preetkaurnanak

Moses & The Promised Land
(Mosè e la Terra Promessa)

"You can see but you cannot enter!"
Said God to Moses.
"But why?"
Screamed Moses.
"I have done everything you have asked of me!"
"Yet, you won't let me in!"
"WHY?"
Screamed Moses as he looked over at The Promised Land.

"Yes, it is true, you have done everything I have asked of you, Moses."
"But you are not worthy!"
"I had decided long before you came upon this highway."
"You fate had already been determined."
"Your destiny sealed."
Said God.
"You were NEVER meant to enter The Promised Land, Moses!"

Sometimes, you can...
...see but you cannot touch.
...touch but you cannot taste.
...taste but you cannot swallow.
...shallow but you cannot enjoy.
...enjoy but you cannot feel.
...feel but you cannot be ALIVE!
...LIVE but you CANNOT enter!
And this is the story of...
...Moses & "The Promised Land!"

"The Don"
16.07.2021

Sex & Friendship

(Sesso e Amicizia)

"So, you put sex before our friendship!"
She said…
…"No!"
I replied.
"For me, sex goes with our friendship!"
"I don't put it above our friendship!"
"But obviously you see this differently."
"You can separate the two.
"I cannot!"
"And that's where the difference lies."

The oldest conflict between sex & friendship!

"Preet Kaur Nanak" (Insta: preetkaurnanak)

The Don"
16.08.2021

Child of the Universe

(Figlia dell'Universo)

We are made of star stuff.
We come from the stars.
We will return to the stars.
We are one & the same.
We are a *"Child of the Universe"!*

That's where we come from.
That's where we belong.
That's where we will end.
That's the where our journey ends.
That's where we started.
We are a *"Child of the Universe"!*

The Universe is inside us.
The Universe is outside us.
We are one & the same.
We are the Universe.
We are a *"Child of the Universe"!*

We are made of star stuff.
We come from the stars.
We will return to the stars.
I am a *"Child of the Universe"!*
You are a *"Child of the Universe"!*
We are a *"Child of the Universe"!*

"I'm a child of South Africa
I'm a child of Vietnam
I'm a child of Northern Ireland
I'm a small boy with blood on his hands
Yes, I'm a child of the universe
Yes, I'm a child of the universe
You can see me on the TV every night
Always there to join in someone else's fight.

"*I'm a child of South Africa*
I'm a child of Vietnam
I'm a child of Northern Ireland
I'm a small boy with blood on his hands
Yes, I'm a child of the universe
Yes, I'm a child of the universe
You can see me on the TV every night
Always there to join in someone else's fight.

I didn't ask to be born and I don't ask to die
I'm an endless dream, a gene machine
That cannot reason why.

Yes, I'm a child of the universe
Yes, I'm a child of the universe
You can see me on the TV every day
I'm the child next door three thousand miles away."

Songwriter: John Lees
Performed by: Barclay James Harvest

"Preet Kaur Nanak
Insta: preetkaurnanak

"The Don"
17.08.2021

The Elder

(L'anziano)

The Elder has the wisdom of the Ages.
The Elder is not defined by...
...gender.
...ethnicity.
...socio-economic background.
...political views.
...age.

But rather is defined by being...
...respectful.
...compassionate.
...friendly.
...kind.
...caring.
...positive.
...optimistic.
...mystical.
...spiritual.
...luminous.

Are you an Elder?

"The Don"
17.08.2021

Are You Experienced?
(Hai Esperienza?)

Do you know what you're doing?
Do you have the touch?
Do you have the skills?
Do you have the feeling?
Do you have the HE♥RT?
Do you have the LO♥E?
Do you have the SOUL?
Are You Experienced?

Have you done this before?
Have you paid your dues?
Have you lived the *"Blues"*?
Have you lived a full life?
Have you tasted the *"Sweet delights"*?
Are You Experienced?

"If you are, can you teach me?"

"Preet Kaur Nanak
Insta: preetkaurnanak

"The Don"
17.08.2021

Nettie

Are you from SETI?
Are you an ALIEN?
You come & go like a ghost.
You appear & then you disappear.
But I know your name...
...*Nettie.*

You are ethereal.
You are a gentle breeze.
You are gossamer wings.
You are an ANCIENT soul.
You are *"The LIGHT"*.
You are Nettie.

She was born near *"Uluru"* in central Australia.
A very important sacred & spiritual site of First Nation Peoples.
It is a place of mystical energy.
Maybe this is why...
...*Nettie is so special.*

I have never been there.
I hope to one day.
Maybe...
...*with Nettie*

"The Don"
17.09.2021

Nettie & Myko
Photo taken by Vito, 18.08.2021

Times

(I Tempi)

They were the *"old Times"*.
These are the *"new Times"*.
That was the *"old Times"*.
This is the *"new Times"*.
The *"Times they are a'changing"*.
I used to care but *"Times have changed"*.
The *"most important challenge of the Times"*.
The *"Olden Times"*.
The *"Golden Times"*.
The *"Future Times"*.
The *"Times of our lives"*.
It's a *"Sign of the Times"*.
It's *"Times like these"*.
It's the *"best of Times"*.
These are *"Modern Times"*.
These are *"The Times we live in"*.
"Those Times".
"Past Times".
"These Times".
"Future Times".

"The Don"
18.08.2021

Whatever Gets You Through the Night (Is Alright!)
(Qualunque Cosa ti Faccia Passare la Notte (Va Bene!))

The Night descends upon us like an eerie mist.
I envelopes me.
It engulfs me.
It consumes me.
It subsumes me.
It shrouds me.
It mystifies me.
It intrigues me.
It bewitches me.
It plays with me
It takes me on new adventures.
Whatever Gets You Through the Night
(Is Alright!)

What adventures will I get into this Night?
Will it be...
...romance (something close to my heart)?
...nostalgia?
...family issues?
...going back to my school days?
...a psychedelic trip that makes no sense.
...binging on NETFLIX?
...having an argument with your boyfriend?
...getting drunk & getting stoned?
...sitting watching the night sky?
...watching the stars & La Luna?
...writing a poem about The Night?
Whatever Gets You Through the Night
(Is Alright!)

"Whatever gets YOU through the Night!"

"It's ALRIGHT!"

"Whatever gets you through the night
It's all right, it's all right
It's your money or your life
It's all right, it's all right
Don't need a sword to cut through' flowers
Oh no, oh no.
Whatever gets you through your life
It's all right, it's all right
Do it wrong, or do it right
It's all right, it's all right
Don't need a watch to waste your time
Oh no, oh no.

Hold me, darlin', come on, listen to me
I won't do you no harm
Trust me, darlin', come on, listen to me
Come on, listen to me, come on, listen, listen.

Whatever gets you to the light
It's all right, it's all right
Out of the blue, or out of sight
It's all right, it's all right
Don't need a gun to blow you mind
Oh no, oh no.

Hold me, darlin', come on, listen to me
I won't do you no harm
Trust me, darlin', come on, listen to me
Come on, listen to me, come on, listen, listen."

Songwriter: John Lennon

"The Don"
19.08.2021

How Old Are You?

(Quanti Anni Hai?)

How old are you?
I'm as old as the oldest tree.
How old are you?
I'm as old as the oldest mountain.
How old are you?
I'm as old as the wind.
How old are you?
I'm as old as the air.
How old are you?
I'm as old as the light.
How old are you?
I'm as old as the stars.
How old are you?
I'm as old as the Cosmos.
How old are you?
I'm as old as the Universe.
How old are you?
I'm as old as GOD.
How old are you?
I'm ae old as infinity.
How old are you?
I'm as old as DEATH.
How old are you?
I'm as old as you imagination.
How old are you?
I'm as old as Time itself.
How old are you?

"How old am I?"

"The Don"
21.08.2021

Manipulation

(Manipolazione)

Everything we do is *Manipulation*.
I *manipulate* you.
You *manipulate* me.
All our actions are a *manipulation*.
It's a law of Nature.
It's because everything is interconnected.
Every action has a consequence.
Every action has repercussions.
Every action is interconnected.
It's like throwing a pebble into a lake.
The ripples the pebble creates are the consequences of its action.
The ripples spread out from the origin.
Spreading far & wide.
Changing everything in its path.
These ripples are our actions.
Spreading out from the origin *(me)* far & wide.
Changing everything in its path.
Influencing everything it touches.
Everything is Manipulation.

"I'm manipulating you now!"

Stella

(Star)

I have a star.
Its name is *"Stella"*.
It looks after me.
It protects me.
It is connected to me.
It LO♥ES me.
My "Stella".

I look for it in the night sky.
Burning so brightly.
Sending out it's light to me.
Talking to me.
Telling me that it is looking out for me.
That it's *"got my back"!*
That everything will be alright.
My "Stella".

We communicate across the cosmos.
She talks to me.
I talk to her.
She is energy.
I am energy.
She is a star.
She is made of *"star stuff"*.
I am made of *"star staff"*.
We are one & the same.
Because I come from her.
I come from the stars too.
Just like my "Stella".

Sometimes I can't see her.
But she's always there.
Night & day.
She's there.
She's permanence.
She's constant.
She NEVER lets you down.
You can count on her.
ALWAYS!
My "Stella".

Do you have a star?
You can have *"Stella"*.
If you want?
She is more than happy to look after you too.
My "Stella".

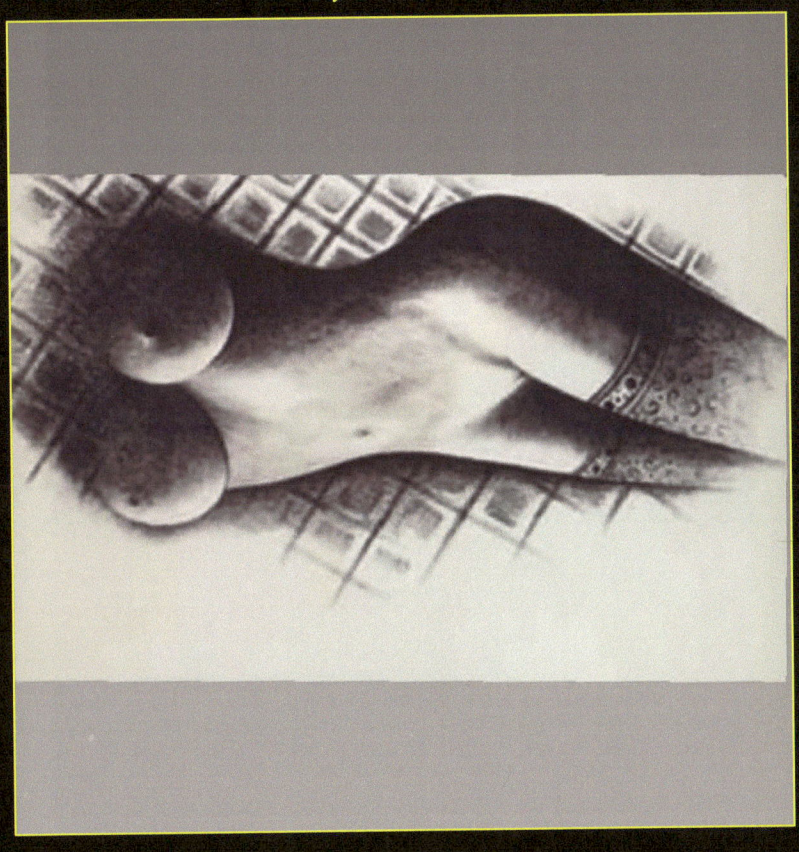

"Preet Kaur Nanak
Insta: preetkaurnanak

"The Don"
23.08.2021

Structure

(Struttura)

Everything is a *"Structure"*.
Everything is a *"Form"*.
Learn the *"Structure"*.
Learn the *"Form"*.
Memorise the *"Structure"*.
Memorise the *"Form"*.
Enact the *"Structure"*.
Enact the *"Form"*.
Embody the *"Structure"*.
Embody the *"Form"*.
Live the *"Structure"*.
Live the *"Form"*.

You are a *"Structure"*.
You are a *"Form"*.

"Structure" is in EVERYTHING
"Form" is in EVERYTHING!

Look for it
Feel it.
Live it!

"The Don"
23.09.2021

Better Out Than In

(Meglio Fuori Che Dentro)

You got shit inside you?
You got troubles on your mind?
You got worries inside you?
You got problems troubling you?
You gotta get them out.
Get them out!
Let them out!
Because...
... *better out than in!*

Be *creative.*
Be *musical.*
Be *artistic.*
Be a *singer.*
Be a *dancer.*
Be a *LO♥ER.*
Be a *poet.*
You gotta get them out.
Get them out!
Let them out!
Because...
... *better out than in!*

Be *joyous.*
Be *happy.*
Be *fun.*
Be *ecstatic.*
Be *ebullient.*
Be *effusive.*
You gotta get them out.
Get them out!
Let them out!
Because...
... *better out than in!*

"I've got a LOT of SHIT inside of me!"
"That's why I'm a poet!"

"The Don"
24.08.2021

The "Why Not" Attitude

(L'atteggiamento del "Perché No")

Why not take a *risk?*
Why not take a *chance?*
Why not take a *leap?*
Why not take a *jump?*
Why not take a *plunge?*
I like the "Why Not" attitude.

Why not have *a go?*
Why not have some *adventure?*
Why not have some *fun?*
Why not have a *laugh?*
Why not have a *dance?*
Why not have a *sing?*
That's the "Why Not" attitude.

"Why Not!"

"What do you have to lose?"

"Preet Kaur Nanak
Insta: preetkaurnanak

"The Don"
25.08.2021

Do Not Seek the Treasure

(Non Cercare il Tesoro)

Do not seek *your fortune*.
Do not seek *money*.
Do not seek *power*.
Do not seek *the diamonds*.
Do not seek *the silver*.
Do not seek *the gold*.
Do not seek *immortality*.
Do not seek the *"Fountain of Youth"*.
Do not seek *"The Promised Land"*.
Do not seek *Heaven*.
Do not seek *HELL*.
Do not seek the *"Treasure"*.

There is no *fortune*.
There is no *money*.
There is no *power*.
There are no *diamonds*.
There is no *gold*.
There is no *immortality*.
There is no *"Fountain of Youth"*.
There is no *"Promised Land"*.
There is no *Heaven*.
There is no *HELL*.
There is no *"Treasure"*.
So...
...do not seek the *"Treasure"*.

"You'll be disappointed!"

"The Don"
25.08.2021

The Perfect Gentleman
(Il Perfetto Gentiluomo)

I never made a move.
I never made an attempt to kiss her.
I was very restrained.
I was the perfect gentleman.

Even when she said, *"I'll never be your bitch!"*
I was cool.
I let it fly by.
I let it go.
I was the perfect gentleman.

I kept my calm.
I was composed.
I was relaxed.
I was in control.
I was the perfect gentleman.

I had help, of course.
Overlooking me.
First there was *"Stella"*.
Then there was *"La Luna"*.
I was the perfect gentleman.

"The Don"
27.08.2021

I'll Be the Judge of That

(Sarò il Giudice di Questo)

You can't do that.
You can't stand there.
You can't sit there.
You can't say that.
You can't think that.
You can't feel that.
I'll be the judge of that.

Don't have a mind.
Don't think.
Don't speak.
Don't act.
Don't feel.
Only when I tell you.
I'll be the judge of that.

Do what I say.
I know best.
You can't think for yourself.
I'll tell you what to think.
Don't feel for yourself.
I'll tell you what to feel.
I know better.
I'll be the judge of that.

I know better than you.
Because...
...I'll be the judge of that.

"Am I TOO judgmental?"

"I'll be the judge of that!"

Inspired from a conversation with Eileen @ "Poet's Corner", Glebe

"The Don"
28.08.2021

I Wish

(Spero che)

I wish for...
...happiness.
...world peace.
...justice.
...political accountability.
...social equity.
...a sustainable future.
...a green planet.
...happiness.
...your HE❤RT.
...LO❤E.
..."Enlightenment".

"It's just a wish!"

"But wishes can come true!"

"Or are my wishes in vain?"

"The Don"
29.08.2021

Low

(Basso)

Keep it low, my *maestra* told me.
Keep it down.
Keep it on the ground.
Keep it low.

Lower it.
Go lower.
Even lower.
Keep it low.

Feel the vibration.
Feel the frequency.
Feel the vibe.
Feel the low.

Keep it lower.
That's the way.
Maintain it.
Sustain it.
Keep it low.

Keep it low.

Keep it low.

Keep it low.

Keep it low.

"The Don"
29.08.2021

Acknowledgement

(Riconoscimento)

We all seek *approval*.
We all seek *praise*.
We all seek *recognition*.
We all seek *attention*.
We all seek *fame*.
We all seek *fortune*.
We all seek *notoriety*.
We all seek *infamy*.
We all seek *conformity*.
We all seek LO♥E.
We all seek acknowledgement.

Do not seek *approval*.
Do not seek *praise*.
Do not seek *recognition*.
Do not seek *attention*.
Do not seek *fame*.
Do not seek *fortune*.
Do not seek *notoriety*.
Do not seek *infamy*.
Do not seek *conformity*.
Do not seek LO♥E.
Do not seek acknowledgement.

"Do you like it?"

"The Don"
31.08.2021

We Were Born to Die

(Siamo Nati per Morire)

Accept that fact.
There's no point struggling against it.
There's no point fighting it
This is our fate.
This is our destiny.
This is our journey.
We were born to DIE.

Accept your fate.
From the moment of birth.
We know we are going to die.
You cannot escape this truth.
You cannot escape this fact.
You cannot escape this fate.
You cannot escape this destiny.
You cannot escape this journey.
We were born to DIE.

Do not struggle against the inevitable.
Do not fight against the inevitable.
Embrace the inevitable.
Embrace your fate.
Accept the inevitable.
Accept your fate.
Face the inevitable
Face your fate.
We were born to DIE.

"Laugh in its face!"
We were born to DIE.

"I'm laughing right now!"

"The Don"
31.08.2021

Shadows in the Night

(Ombre Nella Notte)

Shadows lurking in the darkness.
Shadows hidden by shadows.
Shadows watching.
Shadows waiting.
Shadows hiding.
Shadows afraid to show themselves.
Shadows in the Night.

What are they waiting for?
What are they watching?
What are they looking for?
What are they hiding from?
What are they afraid of?
Shadows in the Night?

Are they lost souls?
Are they ghosts?
Are they spirits?
Are they from another dimension?
Are they from another reality?
Are they from the *"Twilight Zone"*?
Are they from the *"Outer Limits"*?
Are they from the *"X-Files"*?
These shadows in the Night.

"They are all around us."
"What do they want?"

"The Don"
31.08.2021

Suffering

(Sofferenza)

You like to suffer, don't you?
It's your comfort zone.
You understand it.
You wallow in it.
You revel in it.
You look for it.
You want it.
You bring it on yourself.
You want to suffer.
You like suffering.

Suffering is part of you.
Suffering is part of your identity.
Suffering gives you meaning.
Suffering gives you purpose.
Suffering makes you feel alive.
Suffering fills a hole inside you
Suffering fills an emptiness inside you.
Suffering completes you.
Suffering is a type of self-punishment.
Suffering is a type of self-flagellation.
Suffering makes you feel good.

Give me suffering.
I want suffering.
I like suffering.
I enjoy suffering.
I devour suffering.
I am suffering.
I need more suffering.

Give me more suffering.

"I'm suffering right now!"

"The Don"
01.09.2021

We Were Born to Live

(Siamo Nati per Vivere)

We will die that is true.
We will die that is a fact.
We will die that is our fate.
We will die that is our destiny.
We will die, accept this inevitably.
But in-between birth & death...
...we were born to LIVE!

Forget about DEATH.
Don't pay it any mind.
Don't waste your time thinking about the End.
Enjoy the journey.
Enjoy the ride
Enjoy the adventure.
Enjoy your LIFE.
Because...
...we were born to LIVE!

Live every moment like it's the ONLY moment.
Live *"in the moment"*.
Live a full life.
Live a happy life.
Live a complete life.
Live every day like it's your last.
Because...
...we were born to LIVE!

So...
...have fun.
...be happy.
...laugh.
...sing.
...dance.
...be creative.
...LO♥E.
...don't waste a moment.
Because...
...we were born to LIVE!

"Hey, I'm alive & LO♥ING it!"

"The Don"
01.09.2021

In-Sane

(In-Sano di Mente)

I'm completely *In-Sane!*
I have absolutely no *Sanity*.
I'm *irrational*.
I'm *illogical*.
I'm *mad*.
I'm *In-Sane*.

I'm...
...*In-Sanity*.
...*In-Famy*.
...*In-Famous*.
...*Aladdin In-Sane*.
I'm *In-Sane*.

In-Sane is the new Sane.
In-Sane is the new rational.
In-Sane is the new reasonable.
In-Sane is the new logical.
In-Sane is the new normal.
Become *In-Sane* like me.

Sanity is *In-Sane*.
Rational is *In-Sane*.
Logical is *In-Sane*.
Reason is *In-Sane*.
In-Sane is Sanity.

In-Sane is making sense.
In-Sane is thinking.
In-Sane is non-compliance.
In-Sane is non-conforming.
In-Sane is non-conformity.
In-Sane is the way to be.

"Stop being sensible!"
"Stop being sane!"
"Become In-Sane."

"And have a good life!"

"The Don"
01.09.2021

Fantasy & Reality

(Fantasia e Realtà)

What I *"want"* is a FANTASY.
What actually *"happens"* is the REALITY.
My *"desires"* are a FANTASY.
Lust is a FANTASY.
"I want *to be LO♥ED!*" is a FANTASY.
LO♥ING is a REALITY.
Being LO♥ED is a REALITY.
My *"needs"* is a FANTASY.
What I *"get"* is the REALITY.
I *"require"* is a FANTASY.
I *"wish for"* is a FANTASY.
I *"deserve"* is a FANTASY.
I *"must have"* is a FANTASY.
Dreaming is a FANTASY.
Happiness is a FANTASY.
Suffering is a REALITY.
Peace is a FANTASY.
Immortality is a FANTASY.
DEATH is the REALITY.
Do NOT be confused between Fantasy & Reality.

It's so easy to do!

"I'm in a FANTASY right now!"

"Preet Kaur Nanak (Insta: preetkaurnanak)

"The Don"
01.09.2021

I Am a Spirit in the Material World
(Sono Uno Spirito nel Mondo Materiale)

Matter is *energy*.
Energy is *matter*.
I am *matter*.
I am *energy*.
I am *one & the same*.
I am a spirit in the material world.

I am *ethereal*.
I am *anti-matter*.
I am *frequency*.
I am *LIGHT*.
I am *LO❤E*.
I am a spirit in the material world.

"What are you?"

"Preet Kaur Nanak (Insta: preetkaurnanak)

"The Don"
06.09.2021

HUMANISE YOURSELF

(Umanizzare te Stesso)

Become *Humane*.
Become *caring*.
Become *kind*.
Become *gentle*.
Become *empathetic*.
Become *compassionate*.
Become *respectful*.
Become *non-violent*.
Become *non-discriminating*.
Become *Human*
Humanise yourself.

Humanise *politicians*.
Humanise *politics*.
Humanise the *government*.
Humanise *"The Establishment"*.
Humanise *society*.
Humanise the *World*.
Humanise yourself.

"Preet Kaur Nanak (Insta: preetkaurnanak)

"The Don"
06.09.2021

A Hopeful Human

(Un Umano Pieno di Speranza)

I have faith in Humans.
I have faith in Humanity.
I am an optimist.
I am a hopeless optimist.
I am a hopeless Humanist.
I am a hopeful Human.

Humans will survive.
Humanity will prevail.
Humanity always reaches for *"The Light"*.
Humans have been through *"Dark Ages"* before.
I have faith in Humans.
I have faith in Humanity.
I am an optimist.
I am a hopeless optimist.
I am a hopeless Humanist.
I am a hopeful Human.

"What are you?"

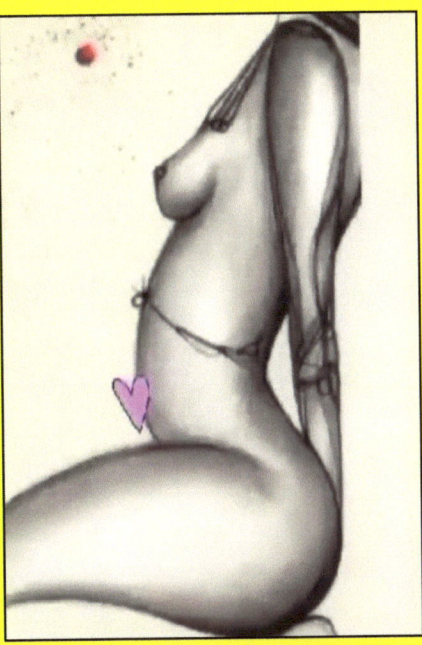

"Preet Kaur Nanak (Insta: preetkaurnanak)

"The Don"
06.09.2021

We Can be LO♥ERS but We Cannot Be Friends
(Possiamo essere Amanti ma non Possiamo essere Amici)

Can we be LO♥ERS & yet not be friends?
So, you only fuck strangers?
I was born to pleasure men.
I gave him everything he wanted.
I will never be your bitch.
I'm a *"mother fucking bitch"*.
I will fuck with you!
I never look back.
I'm not here to stay.
I am not playing my *"A"* game.
I deliver.
"Are you gonna deliver?"
I know I am beautiful.
I know I am desirable.
But I am not going to fuck you.
Because...
...I only fuck strangers.

"We can be friends but we can't be LO♥ERS!"
Because...
...we can be LO♥ERS but we cannot be friends.

"You are my friend."
"I don't fuck my friends!"

"Preet Kaur Nanak (Insta: preetkaurnanak)

"The Don"
06.09.2021

"Preet Kaur Nanak (Insta: preetkaurnanak)

Books written by "The Don"

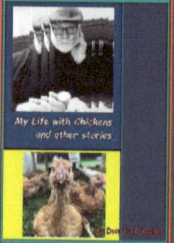
"My Life with Chickens & other stories: I Pity the Poor Immigrant"
Published:
10th September, 2019
Autobiography Book 1:
0 – 12 years old

"Poems for Misfits, Miscreants, Misanthropes, Mavericks, Losers & Malcontents!"
Published:
10th June, 2020
Book of Poems 1

"Poems for Troubled Minds & Trouble Hearts"
Published:
10th August, 2020
Book of Poems 2

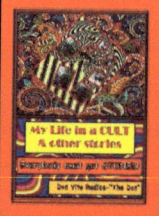
"My Life in a CULT & other stories: Everybody Must Get STONED!"
Published:
10th September, 2020
Autobiography Book 2:
15 – 30 years old

"Poems for Restless Minds & Restless Hearts"
Published:
10th October, 2020
Book of Poems 3

"Poems for Anarchists, Revolutionaries, Outlaws & Dissidents!"
Published:
10th November, 2020
Book of Poems 4

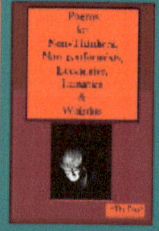
"Poems for Non-Thinkers & Eccentrics"
Published:
10th December, 2020
Book of Poems 5

"The Rantings of a Madman"
Published:
10th January, 2021
Book of Poems 6

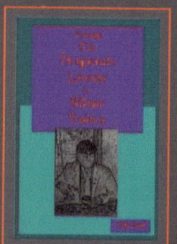
"Poems for Desperate Lovers & Silent Voices"
Published:
10th February, 2021
Book of Poems 7

"Poems for Tormented Minds & Tortured Souls"
Published:
10th March, 2021
Book of Poems 8

All available ONLY online

Books written by "The Don"

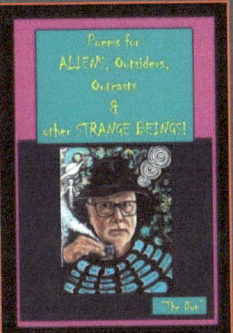

"Poems for ALIENS, Outsiders, Outcasts & other STRANGE BEINGS!"
Published: 10th April, 2021
Book of Poems 9

"Poems for Beings From Another Planet"
Published: 10th May, 2021
Book of Poems 10

"Poems for Mindless Beings & Lost Souls"
Published: 10th June, 2021
Book of Poems 11

"Poems for the Broken Hearted & Misunderstood
Published: 10th July, 2021
Book of Poems 12

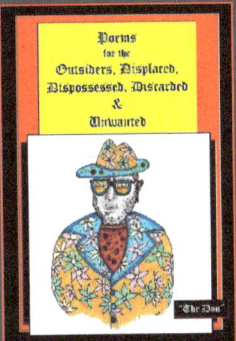

"Poems for Poems for the Bewildered, Dazed & Confused"
10th August, 2021

Book of Poems 13

"Poems for the Outsiders, Displaced, Dispossessed, Discarded & Unwanted"
Published: 10th Sept, 2021
Book of Poems 14

All available ONLY online

"Poems for Secret Agents, Phantom Agents, Agents of Change, Agent Provocateurs & Agents of Chaos"
Published: 10th Oct, 2021
Book of Poems 15

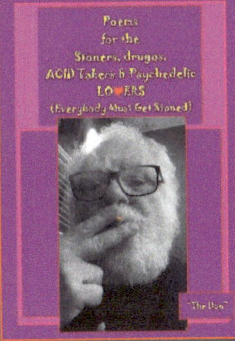

"Poems for the Stoners, drugos, ACID takers & Psychedelic LO♥ERS (Everybody Must Get Stoned)"
Published: 10th December, 2021

Book of Poems 17

Apology:

My deepest apologies to the fantastic artist *Vanessa Wells (Insta: @nesiw_)*, for omitting to cite that she contributed her drawings in my book of poems #14: ***"Poems for the Outsiders, Displaced, Dispossessed, Discarded & Unwanted"***

-"The Don"

"Preet Kaur Nanak (Insta: preetkaurnanak)

Vito Radice ("The Don")
(Poet/Author/Polemicist/Non-Thinker/Non-Intellectual)
Email: vitoradice@gmail.com
Instagram: don_vito_radice
Facebook: Vito Radice
Mobile: +61490012461 (Australia)

www.ingramcontent.com/pod-product-compliance
Lightning Source LLC
Chambersburg PA
CBHW042048290426
44109CB00006B/147